MW01242235

Growth Factor

Seven Keys to Define Your Message, Target the Right Customers, and Win Big in Business

BJ O'Neal

Copyright © 2016 Best Seller Publishing® LLC

All rights reserved. No part of this book may be used or reproduced in any manner whatsoever without prior written consent of the authors, except as provided by the United States of America copyright law.

Published by Best Seller Publishing®, Pasadena, CA

Best Seller Publishing® is a registered trademark

Printed in the United States of America.

ISBN-13:978-1523991976
ISBN-10:1523991976

This publication is designed to provide accurate and authoritative information with regard to the subject matter covered. It is sold with the understanding that the publisher is not engaged in rendering legal, accounting, or other professional advice. If legal advice or other expert assistance is required, the services of a competent professional should be sought. The opinions expressed by the authors in this book are not endorsed by Best Seller Publishing® and are the sole responsibility of the author rendering the opinion.

Most Best Seller Publishing® titles are available at special quantity discounts for bulk purchases for sales promotions, premiums, fundraising, and educational use. Special versions or book excerpts can also be created to fit specific needs.

For more information, please write:

Best Seller Publishing®

1346 Walnut Street, #205

Pasadena, CA 91106

or call 1(626) 765 9750

Toll Free: 1(844) 850-3500

Visit us online at: www.BestSellerPublishing.org

The difference between average people and achieving people is their perception of and response to failure.[1]
– JOHN C. MAXWELL

Growth is the great separator between those who succeed and those who do not. When I see a person beginning to separate themselves from the pack, it's almost always due to personal growth.[2]
– JOHN C. MAXWELL

---

1   John C. Maxwell quote. (n.d.). Retrieved November 30, 2015, from http://www.brainyquote.com/quotes/quotes/j/johncmaxw600862.html

2   John C. Maxwell quote. (n.d.). Retrieved November 30, 2015, from http://www.brainyquote.com/quotes/quotes/j/johncmaxw600889.html

TABLE OF CONTENTS

ACKNOWLEDGEMENTS

I'm thankful to my beautiful wife, DeAundra, for supporting me along the journey of life. She has helped me flesh out the bazillion ideas (you think I'm exaggerating) that I've had throughout our 21-year marriage. Without her support I wouldn't have the ability to follow my passion, which has allowed me to write this book.

I'm also proud to be a John Maxwell Team Founding Partner as a coach, trainer, and speaker. I appreciate the dedication that John Maxwell has for his message of adding value to others and encouraging us all to live a life of significance.

INTRODUCTION

Do you ever feel that you want to grow your business, but you are overwhelmed and unsure of how to get it done? Maybe you would like to start a business, but you don't know exactly where to start. Maybe you are like me; you had businesses in the past where things did not go according to the plan. Or perhaps you have started a business, or you are a marketing director or manager for a business, and things are going great, but you are unsure of how to take it to the next step. Perhaps things have plateaued.

In this book, you will learn seven invaluable business principles (plus a bonus at the end) that can help you potentially double or even triple your income. You will discover some of the techniques and tools that the professionals use that can make all the difference in the world when it comes to marketing, advertising, and building a legitimate business. Most people believe that getting incredible results in advertising and marketing is nearly impossible, until they learn the true techniques on how to get it done.

You will also discover foundations and principles that, if applied correctly, can make all the difference in the world. I believe that these foundations and principles are lacking in the majority of small and medium-sized businesses today because we as a culture want results immediately. While there are a few rule-breakers, most significant businesses took time and take time to develop. Just jumping on the latest and greatest advertising channel will not cut it.

I wrote this book based on the years of conversations I, as a business coach, have had with businesses of all sizes. As a current and previous business owner myself, I know far too well the challenges that entrepreneurs and business owners face. I have personally been through the ups and downs and the good and bad of business ownership. I know the daily grind. It can be extremely challenging to grow a business and see the big picture when you work inside the business every single day. While it can be very time-consuming and even stressful, the rewards of being a business owner or entrepreneur are incredible.

Each chapter of this book is filled with principles and steps on how to take your business to the next level. This book is not designed to give you a quick-rich opportunity, nor is it going to help you double your profits overnight. It is, however, a book that will give you insights and resources regarding the seven main areas businesses desire, but tend to ignore.

If you are interested in building a legitimate business with a solid foundation that is designed to last, then I invite you to read it in its entirety and implement the principles that can make the difference.

Keep your dreams alive. Understand to achieve anything requires faith and belief in yourself, vision, hard work, determination, and dedication. Remember all things are possible for those who believe.[3]

– GAIL DEVERS

---

3 Gail Devers quote. (n.d.). Retrieved November 30, 2015, from http://www.brainyquote.com/quotes/quotes/g/gaildevers144884.html

Chapter 1

THE RIGHT VISION

What exactly is a vision statement? I am often asked about the subject of vision statements, or purpose statements as some may call them. There is a lot of confusion on this topic. Many find it difficult to understand the purpose of a vision statement and how to use it. They fail to grasp what a vision statement can do for their business or company. People are often confused by the words "vision statement." They think that they are just words on paper. Or it's something that people have told them that they need to do to have a legitimate business; "It's what it all the big guys do."

A vision statement is typically a one, two, or maybe even three-sentence-long statement (sometimes more) that describes your desired end state. It forecasts the future of what you or your company wants to become, or what you want to see your company do. It casts a long-term vision of the results that you would like to see. A vision statement often provides direction and inspiration. The best vision statements are clear, memorable, and concise. A vision statement is a layout of an overarching primary goal for any business or company. It's not a detailed plan of how to achieve your vision. It says what you are attempting to achieve. The plan for how to get there will come later.

You may have heard the phrase: "If you don't aim for a target, then you'll hit it every time." That is what often happens when people don't have a vision or when they set a vision that is either unrealistic or doesn't apply. They begin to do things that feel important and might be great ideas but don't point to any vision or purpose for the company.

When you constantly look at your vision statement, it forces you to ask whether or not everything you do fits with your vision. Is what you are doing helping you achieve your goal? Is it helping you to get the result that you set forth?

When I was doing some in-depth research on the vision statements of some of the world's largest companies, I was surprised by how many of them were unclear. There were Fortune 500 companies that had vision statements that didn't say where they were headed or what they were trying to accomplish.

A vision statement is not the same as a mission statement. There is a lot of discrepancy between vision and mission, and when they are confused, it becomes problematic.

Vision statements are future based. They say: "This is what we want to see happen down the road." They are largely about the future of the business or company.

Mission statements are present based. They point to the purpose of the organization, business, or company and their reason for existence. They point towards the overarching goal of a vision. They say: "This is where we want to be, and this is what we want to accomplish down the road."

You may think it's no big deal, but mixing up the two can be a big contributor to losing sight of what you are trying to accomplish if you don't follow the vision.

Everything – and I mean everything – you do should point back to your vision. Every task, every marketing campaign, every person you hire, and every partnership you get involved with should have a filter. You should ask: What am I trying to accomplish? What is my vision? Everything you do should point back to the vision.

The beauty of vision statements is that they are fluid; they can change over time – though you don't want to change them often. If they don't change over time, however, you may lose sight of the growth for your company because our culture changes.

Blockbuster Video was a huge company all throughout the '90s, and they were growing rapidly. They were moving into large and small towns all across the country. They bought out mom-and-pop stores, and they offered great money for these businesses. Then they opened up their large stores, and they were one of the few places where you could rent a VHS or DVD. (Yes, I said VHS!) Remember that machine where the top popped up? I'll never forget when our family bought our first VHS player. It was like we were bringing the theater home. What an awesome experience that was!

Back to our main point. Blockbuster didn't take into consideration what the future of technology could do, and they never shifted their vision to adapt accordingly. They kept operating in a way that was slowly becoming outdated and antiquated.

Meanwhile, a little company called Netflix began to show strength, and they pointed towards the future that operated underneath the digital umbrella.

Then another new company called Redbox began to put kiosks outside grocery stores, Walmarts, Targets, and similar places. I'll never forget telling my wife that I would absolutely never rent a movie standing outside of a grocery store. Wrong!

Blockbuster, unfortunately, didn't shift their vision to get into that arena quickly enough. Eventually, they filed for bankruptcy. As of this writing, they are still around trying to compete, but they have not been successful. Though I don't have any specific insight or knowledge, I believe it's largely due to a lack of adapting their vision and strategy changing along the way to change the result of what they were trying to accomplish. It happens with many companies. Other examples are Kmart and Sears. These examples show us that it's important that we understand that visions can be and should be fluid to some degree.

By the way (I almost wanted to abbreviate that and use BTW, since we live in such a texting society), remember the blue-light special at Kmart back in the day? You didn't know what fun was until you went shopping, and that blue light went off followed by "We have a blue-light special on aisle 9." Those were the days!

VISION CASTING

Vision casting is painting a mental picture of what something is going to look like down the road – forecasting the future and what you are trying to accomplish. It is one of the biggest issues that businesses face.

In coaching clients, I have found that one of the reasons that people don't have a vision yet is that they simply don't want to make it. They are not sure of what it should be. They know what their dreams are, but they are not confident enough that they could ever get to the place of their dreams.

As a result, they exist without direction and an ultimate goal that points them down the road to where they need to be. They don't want to forecast a large goal because they are afraid that they won't move in the direction of that goal and consequently that they will feel like a failure. Most people are afraid of failure. We often avoid it by doing as little as possible so that we are not accountable for much. But without a vision statement, there is nothing to measure whether we are failing or succeeding.

Think about it this way: Did you know that if a jet plane were off course just 1 degree from LAX to JFK, it would put you in the Atlantic ocean? You could be off by as much as 30 miles or more. Aren't you glad pilots have specific directions?

Businesses, entrepreneurs, and leaders need to understand that we have to overcome the fear and get clarity on what we want to accomplish. Even as managers or CEOs of companies, we have to have clarity. We need to write down what we want to see happen. Again, visions are fluid; they could be changed, but we don't want to change them very often.

EXAMPLES OF VISION STATEMENTS

The following are some examples of vision statements belonging to companies that are well known around the globe.

Avon: "The Avon vision is to be the company that best understands and satisfies the product, service and self-fulfillment needs of women globally."[4] Avon is saying that they want to understand the needs of women all around the world and that they are going to offer products that satisfy their need. In one sentence, they were able to communicate clearly what they are trying to accomplish.

Macy's: "Our vision is to operate Macy's and Bloomingdale's as dynamic national brands while focusing on the customer offering in each store location."[5]

---

4   Avon | About Us | Contact Us |. (n.d.). Retrieved November 17, 2015, from http://www.my.avon.com/PRSuite/aboutus_landing.page

5   Douglas, E. (2013, July 30). Leading Resources, Inc. Retrieved November 17, 2015, from http://leading-resources.com/strategic-planning/vision-statement-examples-from -high-performing-organizations/

Microsoft: "A personal computer in every home running Microsoft software."[6] That is very short and clear, so there is no misunderstanding of what Microsoft is trying to do.

Alzheimer's Association: "Our vision is a world without Alzheimer's."[7]

Habitat for Humanity: "A world where everyone has a decent place to live."[8] They claim that their goal is to see that everyone has a home. It's very short and sleek. Notice that they are not saying how they are going to get there. They make it very clear what they are trying to accomplish.

Make-A-Wish Foundation: "Our vision is that people everywhere will share the power of a Wish."[9]

The Santiago Zoo: "To become a world leader at connecting people to wildlife and conservation."[10] When you think of a zoo, you probably think of seeing some animals and possibly some shows. However, The Santiago Zoo has made the decision that they also want to be the world leader at connecting people to wildlife. That allows them to do other things within the context of their business model and industry. They are not saying that they want to be a destination where people could come and pet and enjoy animals. That would be a constricting vision compared to the one they have. As it is, they want to be a world leader and be known for helping people connect with animals and conservation. And they are doing a very good job of it because they are one of the best in the world.

Toms Shoes. This company has one of the most unique business models around. Their model is that when you buy a pair of shoes, they give a pair

---

6   Douglas, E. (2013, July 30). Leading Resources, Inc. Retrieved November 17, 2015, from http://leading-resources.com/strategic-planning/vision-statement-examples-from -high-performing-organizations/

7   Help End Alzheimer's. (n.d.). Retrieved November 17, 2015, from http://www.alz.org/

8   Habitat for Humanity International mission statement and principles. (2012, July 16). Retrieved November 17, 2015, from http://www.habitat.org/how/mission_statement.aspx

9   Make-A-Wish® Central California: Frequently Asked Questions. (n.d.). Retrieved November 17, 2015, from http://centralca.wish.org/content/faq

10   Overview. (n.d.). Retrieved November 17, 2015, from http://www.sandiegozooglobal.org/overview

of shoes to someone in need in a third-world country. It's a beautiful model where someone can get something and give something at the same time. They have a different vision than most other shoe manufacturers. They have the vision to provide shoes to those who can't afford them. This vision statement is completely different than Macy's, whose vision is solely to sell shoes. There is nothing wrong with that, but Macy's is going to sell the shoes the traditional way whereas Toms Shoes has a vision of selling shoes for a greater reason and purpose. That is how and why vision statements belonging to companies in the same field can vary greatly.

Back in World War II, there was a troupe leader who was a field marshal. His name was Bernard Montgomery. He was called the soldiers' general. He wrote:

> [E]very single soldier must know, before he goes into battle, how the little battle he is to fight fits into the larger picture, and how the success of his fighting will influence the battle as a whole.[11]

Montgomery knew that he needed to have direction and understand his troupes. Some soldiers could get weary, some could get tired, and some could get frustrated. Some might want to quit because they only saw the little pieces of the activity that they were doing. Without seeing the true vision, the soldiers could forget that the little things that they did – the small fights and battles they fought – were helping the plan of trying to win a war.

That is exactly what a vision statement does; it enables us to follow a plan. It helps us to see that the small tasks, activities, and partnerships are contributing to the overall purpose and vision of what we are trying to accomplish.

HOW TO WRITE A VISION STATEMENT

While there are plenty of ways to write a vision statement, I will outline five steps that are simple ways to encapsulate what you are trying to accomplish and where you are trying to head.

---

11 Maxwell, J. (2011, January 17). Leadership Wired Blog. [Web log post]. Retrieved November 17, 2015, from http://www.johnmaxwell.com/blog/finding-a-visions-true-north

Step 1: Describe the future. Describe what you would like to see happen in 5 or 10 years from now. Don't worry about how to get there. Don't worry about if you have the resources to do it at the moment because you probably don't. That is the purpose of vision casting.

Step 2: Dream big and focus on success. The word "big" means just that. Dream big; don't be held back within your current confines. Perhaps you have 100 customers at the moment, and you want 10,000 customers. You may have no idea how to get 10,000, but don't worry about that. If you know that 10,000 is the number that you want to get to, then write it down, dream big, and focus on success.

Step 3: Write in future tense. In other words, "In five years, our company would like to see 10,000 customers by doing X, Y, Z." If you stay in the present tense, you are more likely to write a vision that you are already achieving. Without writing in the future tense, you are not going to stretch yourself, and you must stretch yourself to get to a goal that is down the road.

Step 4: Paint a graphic mental picture. When the Alzheimer's Association says, "Our vision is a world without Alzheimer's,"[12] we know how to imagine that. I have family members who have passed away from this disease. Many people are connected to somebody who suffers from it. When they say, "a world without that disease," we can visualize that. Set up your vision by painting a graphic mental picture.

Step 5: Start long, and then condense it. When you put your thoughts on paper, use as many paragraphs as you need. Then begin to scale back down to one to three sentences. Truthfully, the shorter it is, the sweeter, clearer and easier it is for you to remember it. Keeping it short also makes it more likely that you, your employees, and your partners are going to adopt it. When a vision statement becomes long, it's harder to connect with it, which is what you want to avoid. Sometimes you need a little more time to express what you try to accomplish, and that is okay, however, one to three sentences is the best format.

Don't fall into the trap that most businesses do where they start running their business before they know where they are headed. Many entrepreneurs have a deep desire to own their own business and be the boss, which is

---

12   Help End Alzheimer's. (n.d.). Retrieved November 17, 2015, from http://www.alz.org/

awesome. However, without establishing a vision first, you do run the risk of missing a lot of opportunities. You might encounter issues that could cause some significant trouble growing the business at all. You have probably heard the statement that 80% of businesses fail in their first year. That is largely due to a lack of a plan. There is no vision or purpose. That is why it's important to have a vision statement.

I just met with a local business owner recently, and I asked him how he got started because I wanted to hear his story. He said: "I started small with no plan. I just did it, and it grew from there." While that works for him and certainly has worked for others, they aren't in the majority. Then I asked him what was the biggest frustration that he currently faces. He said that it bothers him that after nearly 10 years in his community, some people still say that they have never heard of him. I asked him: "Are you following a long-term vision to see your business have exponential growth?" The answer was no. Without a plan, you are sure to hit it every time!

Plan now, and use Stephen Covey's Habit 2 from his book *The 7 Habits of Highly Effective People,* which is to "Begin with the end in mind." What does the end look like? Where would it be?

Once you have written a vision statement, it's important that you integrate it into the everyday culture of your business. That way, everything that you do contributes to that vision. When I say everything, I mean everything!

Most businesses think that product is the most important thing, but without great leadership, mission and a team that deliver results at a high level, even the best product won't make a company successful.[13]

– ROBERT KIYOSAKI

13   Robert Kiyosaki quote. (n.d.). Retrieved November 30, 2015, from http://www. brainyquote.com/quotes/quotes/r/robertkiyo626926.html

Chapter 2

THE RIGHT MISSION

Recently, I sat down with a coaching client to discuss an idea that he needed clarity on. He wanted to talk through it, get my thoughts on it, and find some direction. After we had had a good conversation about his idea, and I had gotten a grasp of what it was, he wanted me to put together some thoughts based on that and then meet up again to review what I had put together. From there, he wanted us to create a plan of action.

Over the following couple of weeks, I sat down and plotted out the concepts of what he was attempting to accomplish. Then I made sure that this idea would not derail him but instead be a help to continue moving him towards his ultimate goal.

When we came back together, he began to share some additional thoughts. I quickly realized that his idea had morphed into something much larger than what we had originally discussed.

This business owner, like a lot of entrepreneurs, loves talking about ideas but has to work hard at staying focused on getting those things accomplished. A lot of great thinkers and visionaries suffer from the "Shinny object syndrome." They can't complete an idea because another one popped up!

To help him get some clarity, I began asking him some questions. As we talked about what he was trying to do, I thought that it was a great idea if he could pull it off. The problem was that it was not connected to or in harmony with the mission that he had previously laid out. Not only was it not in harmony with his mission statement; it wasn't helping him get to his ultimate goal as laid out in his vision statement.

We discussed vision statements in the last chapter. In this chapter, we will look at not just having a mission statement but having the *right mission* statement.

As the business owner and I talked, I pointed out that though it was a good idea, my fear was that it would take him away from his predetermined mission and vision. He shared that he wanted to execute the idea nevertheless, so we discussed it further, and we reached some conclusions.

Our conversation helped me realize that many people don't focus enough on their vision and mission. As a result, they get into rabbit trail ideas. Even though these could be good ideas, they might not be in harmony with the mission and the vision that they have already set out. This is one of the reasons why people don't see their ultimate goals come to fruition; they spend too much time doing things that are not in harmony with what they originally set out to do.

WHAT A MISSION STATEMENT IS

We use the words "mission statement" a lot, but what do they mean? A mission statement is by definition a formal summary of the values of a company, organization, or individual. It points to the vision that you have for the company, and it helps clarify the current purpose of your company. A company's mission statement is a constant reminder to its employee(s) of why the company exists. It exists to create purpose and meaning. A business without purpose can easily become a chore and a pain.

Many people wonder why they feel a sense of purposelessness with their business. It's often because they have not been doing the activities that point to the values of what they originally set out to do when they started the business or company. Without stating the mission, it can easily become lifeless.

Two businesses in the same industry can have very different purposes or reasons for their existence. Take, for example, two real estate brokerage firms. One could be very driven by and focused on profit, and there is nothing wrong with that. The passion and purpose of the other company could be to help single moms find affordable housing to buy or rent. Both are real estate companies. Both buy, sell, and possibly rent properties, but one's purpose is entirely different than the other's.

If the purpose of the real estate company is to find affordable housing for single moms, and they begin to focus on buying, selling, and flipping properties, it doesn't fit with their overarching mission. Then they lose their mission of what they originally wanted to accomplish.

If you are a startup, an investor (even if it is your Aunt Mary) might ask you: "What is the driving purpose behind your business? Why do you want to do this? What is the reasoning?" You need to be prepared to make a compelling case and answer those questions.

THE DIFFERENCE BETWEEN A VISION STATEMENT AND A MISSION STATEMENT

We discussed the difference between a vision statement and a mission statement in the last chapter, but it's extremely critical that you get this part right. Again, the easiest way to remember the difference is that *vision statements are future based*. They are about the goals and where you're headed. *Mission statements are present based*. They are about the values purpose and meaning. Visions cast the dreams and goals. Missions say who you are and why you exist while pointing to your visions, goals, and dreams. Let's look at some examples of mission statements.

The company Life Is Good has become a very successful retailer of clothing and other types of merchandise. As a part of its foundation is the mission of giving back to others. They made a very clear distinction of what their mission is. It is as follows:

> The Life is Good Kids Foundation partners with leading childcare organizations to positively impact the quality of care delivered to the most vulnerable children.[14]

Their vision statement, however, is: "a world where all children grow up feeling safe, loved and joyful."[15] We can see that they have done a very good job of having a goal, which is their vision, and a mission, why they exist. That "why" is helping them to achieve a world where all children grow up feeling safe, loved, and joyful.

---

14   Kids Foundation | Life is good. (n.d.). Retrieved November 17, 2015, from http://content.lifeisgood.com/kidsfoundation/

15   Flutter. (n.d.). Retrieved November 17, 2015, from https://www.experienceflutter.com/charities/life-is-good-playmakers

Google's mission is: "to organize the world's information and make it universally accessible and useful."[16]

Apple has the following mission:

Apple is committed to bringing the best personal computing experience to students, educators, creative professionals and consumers around the world through its innovation hardware, software and Internet offerings.[17]

Apple's mission includes some very specific elements as to how they are going to deliver the best personal computing experience. In the last chapter, we discussed Microsoft's vision statement, which is: "to bring a personal computer into everyone's home."[18] Technically, that could also be Apple's vision. Apple is saying that they are to be committed to the personal computing experience, but they get specific by talking about students, educators, and creative professionals.

As an example of a mission statement of a smaller business, let's look at the one belonging to Allensburg's Food and Gas:

The mission of Allensburg's Food and Gas is to offer commuters on Highway 310 competitive gas prices and great food. The company will make a healthy profit for its owners and provide a rewarding work environment for its employees.[19]

Another example is Integrity Auto Sales:

Integrity Auto Sales provides a unique car buying experience to the customers in the Willamette Valley. One that focuses on customer satisfaction first. We understand that vehicle purchasing is a necessary, but sometimes unpleasant experience. Our goal is to provide the customer

16 Company – Google. (n.d.). Retrieved November 17, 2015, from http://www.google.com/about/company/

17 Apple - Press Info - Media Alert. (n.d.). Retrieved November 17, 2015, from https://www.apple.com/pr/library/2000/04/14Media-Alert.html

18 Douglas, E. (2013, July 30). Leading Resources, Inc. Retrieved November 17, 2015, from http://leading-resources.com/strategic-planning/vision-statement-examples-from-high-performing-organizations/

19 Convenience Store Gas Station Business Plan. (n.d.). Retrieved November 17, 2015, from http://www.bplans.com/convenience_store_gas_station_business_plan/executive_summary_fc.php

with an enjoyable, honest service by satisfying individual customers' practical transportation needs with a quality product.[20]

I like that statement because they have highlighted the fact that there is a black eye in the automotive industry, and they have incorporated that issue into their mission. They are taking an issue in their industry head on.

The mission statement reminds the business owner and everyone involved why they exist. In the example of Integrity Auto Sales, they say flat out that the car-buying experience can be unpleasant sometimes. For that reason, they as a company will change that. When people buy a vehicle there, they will get the opposite; they will get honest service, and they will be satisfied. They will also get a quality product. Sometimes bringing those scenarios into your mission statement can provide great context for the employees.

HOW TO WRITE A MISSION STATEMENT

There are various ways to write a mission statement. Here are five simple steps I believe can help you do it.

Step 1: Begin with the vision statement. Write your vision statement first. That way, when you write a mission statement, it's pointing to your overall goal – your vision statement. This is what people tend to miss. They feel that they have a purpose for their company, so they will write a mission, but they haven't clarified what they are ultimately trying to achieve.

Step 2: Brainstorm for clarity. You need to have a brainstorming session to get clarity on what you want your company to be about. You want to ask clarifying questions like:

- Who are our customers?
- What is our target demographic?
- What do we actually do?
- What value do we add?
- What value do we provide?

---

20   Used Auto Sales Business Plan. (n.d.). Retrieved November 17, 2015, from http://www.bplans.com/used_auto_sales_business_plan/executive_summary_fc.php

These types of questions will help shape what you want to be and how you want to do it. You want to ask many of those kinds of questions to help clarify what you want to do and exactly how you will try to do it.

Step 3: Fight the urge to use qualitative verbiage. Many businesses use phrases like, "to provide the highest customer service," or "deliver the best values in the industry." Sometimes we don't even know what that means. In our earlier example of the Integrity Auto Sales, they clarified that because they said that it could be an unpleasant experience to buy a car.

Sometimes when we use phrases such as "we just want to provide highest customer service," we may wonder who is setting that standard. One person's opinion of customer service can be very different than somebody else's opinion of customer service. When you write vague statements, it can sometimes be difficult to measure your ultimate and overall effectiveness.

Cory Eridon, who is a writer for *Hub Spot Blogs,* once gave the example of Southwest Airlines. Their current mission statement is:

The mission of Southwest Airlines is dedicated to the highest quality of customer service delivered with a sense of warmth, friendliness, individual pride, and company spirit.[21]

Eridon said that if he had written it, he would have said something like this:

Southwest Airlines' mission is all about customer service. Not just any kind of customer service – but high-quality customer service – whether at ticketing, on the plane, in the terminal, and even on our website. This should come through in all places.[22]

Sometimes, getting a little more specific about how and even where you are going to deliver customer service helps clarify the mission for the entire company, leadership, employees, and everyone involved. The goal is to be as clear as possible.

---

21   About Southwest. (n.d.). Retrieved November 17, 2015, from https://www.southwest.com/html/about-southwest/

22   Eridon, C. (2013, June 4). How to Write a Fluff-Free Mission Statement. [Web log post]. Retrieved November 17, 2015, from http://blog.hubspot.com/marketing/fluff-free-mission-statements

Step 4: General guidelines

Your statement should:

- Be short and sweet
- Express your organization's purpose and meaning
- Be clear in a way that people easily understand it
- Motivate you and your employees

Remember that you should use verbs to describe what you do and avoid fluff.

Step 5: Condense your brainstorming material. In the brainstorming session, write down as many sentences as possible based on the above, and then bring it all together. Remember that when you are in a brainstorming session, you will write down things that don't make sense or things that you know are not going to work. That is okay. It's a part of the exercise to get it all out and on a board. Then you can see it and begin to clarify the sentences that describe who you are and what you want to do.

Once you have done that, you can bring it down to several different sentences. Maybe you have two or three different types of mission statements. If you have people around you who could share their wisdom, you can get some advice from them. Sometimes you simply need to read those mission statements over and over for several weeks. Over time, it will begin to click, and you will know in your gut who you ultimately want to become.

The goal is not just to write a mission statement; don't write a mission statement only because it's a part of the business plan. The core reason why the mission statement exists is so that you can make sure that you are providing what your company should provide and remind your employees, partners, and everybody involved exactly why you do what you do.

We all have a life story and a message that can inspire others to live a better life or run a better business. Why not use that story and message to serve others and grow a real business doing it?[23]

– BRENDON BURCHARD

23   Brendon Burchard quote. (n.d.). Retrieved November 30, 2015, from http://www.brainyquote.com/quotes/quotes/b/brendonbur487231.html

Chapter 3
THE RIGHT MESSAGE

Most people don't realize that we have to have a crystal clear message to communicate to those we are trying to sell our products or services to.

Research has shown that we as consumers see about 5,000 messages daily through logos, brands, and advertising campaigns. That is a lot of different logos and imaging! Of those 5,000, somewhere between 250 and 600 are actual advertising messages that push people's brands or specific campaigns. That means that there is a lot of clutter.

No matter what we do, we are all consumers. When it comes to our business or whatever we try to sell, the questions are:

- What are we going to say?
- How are we going to say it?
- How will we present our message to engage people?

A lot of businesses, especially small and medium-sized businesses, don't invest the proper amount of time, effort, and energy to make sure that they have the right message.

As consumers, we notice advertisements and campaigns that have the right messages for us. We notice advertisements that speak to our interests and current desires. So if we are creating messages, the question is: Are we creating messages that resonate with the right people so that they will buy our products or services at some point?

I have been a huge fan of Apple computers for seven years. About seven years ago, I bought my first MacBook Pro. Since then, I have bought an iPod, an iPad, and an iPhone, and now I have an Apple watch. These products fit my lifestyle. I also like the covers for the computers and phones and the different gadgets and gizmos that come along with these products. The companies that market the after-market products for Apple devices understand how a consumer like myself thinks. They know how things need to look in magazine articles, online, or wherever because they always grab my attention.

As a small or medium-sized business, we might not always have the financial resources to do focus group studies and such. But if we don't do something to turn up the heartbeat of our target audience, then we will never put out a message that communicates to their core and engages them.

We must know how to engage and communicate with our customers so that we can create the right message. There are messages, and then there are the *right messages*. Our goal is to create the right messages for our businesses, and that is not a simple thing to do. It's not going to be done in an afternoon by writing down some things and brainstorming on a piece of paper. It takes time. It takes bouncing some ideas off of other people who are experts in the fields of what we try to do. We have to be diligent about making sure that our message is clear and concise and that it resonates with the people we are trying to engage.

Marketing used to be about creating campaigns that drove transactions. Back in the day, there were not many ways to spread messages other than through mass resources. Then marketing was all about creating campaigns that would drive a specific and very simple transaction.

Now it's completely different. Today it's all about establishing relationships with the consumers. All of our marketing initiatives have to harmonize to bring the customers to the final decision, which is the transaction. Everything we do has got to speak to that same thing.

We have to look at all the touch points that our customers experience to make sure that they are truly engaging with our message. That is not an easy thing to do, and sometimes we have to pivot, make changes, and adapt.

One of the important factors of creating a message is making sure that it is clear and concise. Sometimes we have to get our message out in the marketplace to find out if it is working or not. I often see businesses spend a significant amount of time and energy creating their message, and they think that they have perfected it, but when they put it in the marketplace, it simply doesn't do what they had hoped it would do. To avoid that, we have to begin evaluating what kind of feedback we get. Then we should make changes accordingly to see the results that we look for.

Back in 1997, Taco Bell began its famous advertising campaign with its Taco Bell Chihuahua. The famous catchphrase was "!Yo Quiero Taco Bell!" Remember that? This is one of the most successfully recognized advertising campaigns in my lifetime. For three years, that dog was the face of the franchise. There were stuffed animals, coffee mugs, t-shirts, etc.

Did you know that the campaign didn't work? The message may have been funny, but Taco Bell's sales dropped 6% in the second quarter of 2000, and that was the largest such decline in Taco Bell history. They not only ended the campaign, but they also removed the president, *all because of the wrong marketing message.*[24]

Millions of dollars were spent on this campaign. Everyone knew about it, even enough to remember it to this day. However, it failed to connect with customers for one primary purpose: to sell more tacos.

COMMON MISTAKES

The following are three big mistakes I see businesses make when they trying to craft their message. We want to make sure that we avoid these!

Copying others. We should not copy others even though they have successful marketing messages. Just because a competitor who sells a product similar to ours has success in it, it doesn't mean that we should try to do the same thing. I see it happen a lot. Businesses will attempt to copy, if not verbatim, someone else because they saw the success they had, and they hope that they will produce the same results by creating a similar message.

Radio Shack did this back in 2009. As reported in *Inc. Magazine,* Radio Shack wanted to shed the image they had from having been around for a long time. So in an attempt to look and feel like Apple and Best Buy, they decided to drop the name "Radio" from Radio Shack.

They came up with a campaign that was simply called The Shack. Then they developed TV advertisements and billboard campaigns that were close to their retail locations. They hoped that by moving away from the word "Radio," they would open up consumers' perception of what the store sold and let them compete more effectively with the powerhouses in their industry.

---

24   Taco Bell chihuahua. (n.d.). Retrieved November 25, 2015, from https://en.wikipedia.org/wiki/Taco_Bell_chihuahua

It didn't work. The failure of the campaign was evident in their financial findings afterward, where they posted a $53 million loss. The campaign didn't work because it had no uniqueness, and it was more about trying to be like someone else.

Focusing on brand awareness instead of the message. The next thing we have to do is remove the temptation to focus on brand awareness instead of the message. Brand awareness is clearly critical, but businesses will often have their logos and branding all over without centering it on a message. Then they won't be able to create the harmony that we talked about earlier.

We need brand awareness, but we must also think about the message. Companies like McDonald's and other large entities that put up their logos without a message can do that because they are spending millions of dollars to get it out through all kinds of campaigns. They have a significant amount of brand awareness detached from their message.

Making the message all about us. Another mistake that we have to avoid is making the message all about us. We often want to tell our story and say how great we are. We might have the best, biggest, greatest, latest, and flashiest products or business in the world, but no one ultimately cares. We may have the lowest prices in town; no one cares. We may have the best of whatever it is that we sell. Ultimately, no one cares.

When we put our message out into the marketplace, we have to make sure that we make it about the consumer. When we focus on the consumer versus focusing on how we are better and bigger, we significantly increase our opportunity to be successful. Focusing on how we are better and bigger is much like the campaigns that used just to drive transactions. It follows the old model that we have to move away from.

HOW TO CREATE THE RIGHT MESSAGE

There are many different ways to create your message successfully. The following are three simple ways you can do it. Even if you do nothing else but these three things, you will still give yourself a significant opportunity to succeed.

Understand your customer. You have to understand your customer and target demographic. You must do whatever it takes to understand exactly how they think, walk, and talk. Without that understanding, it is extremely difficult to craft a message that will engage them and build a relationship with them.

If you are limited on resources, at least begin engaging with your current customers and ask them questions. Do surveys through email or whatever way you can get in front of them to begin gathering some data. Find out how they think, talk, and walk. Learn about their family life. All these things matter greatly in understanding them.

When you have a true understanding, you will be able to speak their language. That helps tremendously in your communication with them and building a bridge with them.

Identify their pains and needs. We all have struggles, and we all have pains and problems. We are not necessarily always looking for the biggest, best, and the lowest price of anything. Deep down, we are looking for someone to solve our problems. Most people are willing to pay more for the person who can solve a problem than just make a cold transaction. When you identify the pains and needs of your target audience, you can make your message stand out far more in their world because now you can solve their problem.

Find the right words. When you understand your customer and know what their pains are, you can begin to think about how to articulate your message.

Think about the words you choose in terms of how you would write billboard messages. When you advertise on billboards, you don't want to use more than six words because you only have a few seconds of people's attention as they drive by.

If you were to say something in six words or less, what would it be? The way to do that is using common short words that are easily identifiable. Don't try to be impressive with your extended vocabulary. Fewer syllables always sell more that more because they are easier to see and process.

We must always make sure that we say "you" at least twice as much as we say "I." If we say "I" all the time, it becomes all about us.

We want to use words that have warmth and involve emotional responses. Those are the words that help you engage your customers and build relationships with them. You want people to have warm and fuzzy feelings about you. Create images with words. Use action verbs instead of nouns. That is how people craft the message for billboard campaigns.

Those are three simple ways to help you create your message successfully. While there are many other ways to do it, those three will be a great help. The way you express your message – the way you say it, the way it looks, the way it feels – will matter greatly to the people you try to engage.

You need your customer to engage with you through the entire cycle of the experience of your business. The more you can identify who they are, understand them, solve their problems, and make sure that you are unique, the greater advantage you will have. You set yourself up for success by having a clear and simple message that stands out and speaks their language.

Great companies that build an enduring brand have an emotional relationship with customers that has no barrier. And that emotional relationship is on the most important characteristic, which is trust.[25]

– HOWARD SCHULTZ

25 Howard Schultz quote. (n.d.). Retrieved November 30, 2015, from http://www.brainyquote.com/quotes/quotes/h/howardschu592282.html

Chapter 4

THE RIGHT TARGET MARKET

Have you ever had a conversation with someone, and you simply didn't feel like you were connecting with that person? Maybe you began to talk to someone at a party or some event, and you could tell that you weren't on the same page. There were awkward moments and pauses, so you found yourself looking for a way to get out of the conversation because it was simply uncomfortable.

Connecting with people from a human behavior perspective is critical to building a relationship. You have probably seen the dating websites where they help match people based on their personality types and behaviors. There are even niche websites within the dating industry. Maybe you have heard of FarmersOnly.com. This website has become extremely popular.

Now, why wouldn't the people who are interested in dating websites just use eharmony.com? It's because there is a value to being on the same page. That is how you truly connect with someone. Those who are in the farming industry have very specific needs, wants, and desires. When they connect with someone with similar values, likes, needs, and desires, then there will be better communication and so on.

The same principles apply when it comes to finding the right customers for your business. In this chapter, we will discuss how to connect with the perfect market for your business.

Years ago, I sold radio air time for a top 40 radio station in Saint Louis, Missouri. During the first months of my time there, I was in training. One day, I was out with another sales representative, and we had an appointment with a local bar owner. We sat in the bar owner's office, and we discussed opportunities for how we could work together.

After we had talked for a bit, the owner leaned over the desk and said: "I like what I'm hearing, but I have just one big problem with this." I was taken off guard because the conversation up to that point had seemed to go very well. We were connecting; there was good body language, and it seemed like there was good chemistry. He continued: "My problem is, personally, I can't stand the music that you play."

Remember, I was new to radio sales at this point. A part of me thought that right then and there, the conversation had come to an abrupt close, and I was quickly trying to think how to sell an advertising campaign to this guy who had just told us that he hated the music that we played.

My friend was the senior sales representative at that time, and he was and extremely knowledgeable and experienced in radio sales. In a very calm fashion, he leaned up on the desk and said: "With all due respect, I really couldn't care less if you personally like our music or not. What I care about is that my listeners and your customers are the same. Your customers listen to my station. Therefore, my listeners are your perfect customers. And other people who are listening to my station who have never heard of you would love to come to your establishment."

I was blown away by this response. Looking at the gentleman who owned the bar, I saw an expression of extreme surprise and slight shock. It seemed that all these years, he had never thought about what my friend had just said. It was as if he had never realized that something he personally liked could be very different from what his customers would like. It was an eye-opening moment for both of us. I then fully understood that every single thing about our brand and our business or company has to connect to our target audience, not necessarily us.

Ultimately, it doesn't matter what you like. What matters are the preferences of those who will buy your products or services. Everything about the brand – the colors, the way it works, the experience – all of it matters more to your target audience than it does to you, the entrepreneur, business owner, those who work for you or with you, or your vendors or partners.

I can't begin to tell you how many conversations with those who own and manage businesses include the phrase "I don't like that." We have to know right off the bat that to get great results, we have to distinguish what we like from what our customers like. That is a big challenge for some people. Some have always thought about what they want to do and what they like. Again, it doesn't matter what you like. The real questions are: Is it going to work for your target? Is it going to attract the type of customers that you are attempting to get in front of?

CREATE YOUR IDEAL CUSTOMER

Your ideal customer is the person who would make your business explode if you had a thousand of them. To create this ideal customer, customer avatar, or customer profile, you have to sit down and spend some time asking yourself questions about the person who you want to connect with – the person who might buy your products or services.

Here are some questions you can ask:

- What is the ideal age of my customer?
- What is the ideal age range of my customer?
- What are the types of things they are interested in?
- What kind of cars do they drive?
- What is their typical income?
- Are they male or female?

You want to have a great idea of who your customers are. Are they predominantly male or female? Are they typically over or under 35? What would their average income be? These are called qualifying questions. The answers to these questions should dictate the way you view your business and run it.

What type of pains do your customers have? If you know the pains, how can you solve those pains? When you can begin to solve people's problems, you are golden. It's the holy grail of adding value to your customers. When you learn their needs, wants, and drives, you can identify potential problems in their life, and your services or your products begin to solve those problems. It is only when you begin to attract that perfect target that you have a great match, as we discussed at the beginning of this chapter.

Once you have created your customer avatar, then and only then can you begin to make the best decisions regarding brand management and marketing campaigns.

A common mistake that business owners and entrepreneurs make when it comes to finding their target audience is that they are too general. Let's say the owner of a car dealership says that their target market is anyone who owns or needs a car. Well, that is wrong. It's wrong because there are many different demographics among those who will purchase a car.

For example, I can't afford a $500,000 Rolls Royce, but there are people out there who can. (By the way, if I could spend $500,000 on a car, I would be rockin' a sleek black Lamborghini with paddle shifters.)

If a Rolls Royce company markets to me, guess what, they will attract the wrong person. Those who purchase trucks might also have special interests or work needs of a certain demographic. Plenty of ranchers and farmers need trucks for their work. I also know people who own hybrid vehicles. Not only do they want to save on auto fuel, but they also care about the environment. They love to recycle. How you market to someone like that is going to be very different than how you would market to someone who will drive a V8 truck that uses a significant amount of fuel. Understanding those differences helps you define your target.

Let's say that you are a dentist. What type of dentist are you? What is your specialty? What are the things that you do? I know a dentist in my area who has a grand piano and a waterfall in the lobby. Obviously, they cater to a higher-end customer. They want to create an experience beyond just cleaning your teeth. Understanding these things helps you know what the look, overall feel, and experience of their business should be.

If you are a pediatric dentist, your avatar (customer profile) is most likely going to be a woman between 21 and 45 years of age. This age range could be adjusted based on further research in your specific market. Also, your avatar may be a mom with kids mainly at the ages 16 and younger. After a little research, you would perhaps find out that your perfect customer drives a crossover vehicle or possibly a minivan.

Let's say your business is located in an upscale part of your city. You can learn more about incomes based on the area studies that you can find about your local market. Let's assume that in your county or city, the medium household income is $80,000 to $100,000 or more. Now you are getting more and more knowledge of who will buy your products and services.

Once you have this knowledge of your target audience, you center everything about your business on that knowledge. That includes the way you market your business, how you would talk on your social media channels, and the types of social media channels that you use. It also includes the colors of your logo, the placement of your logo, and the way your website looks. Knowing your audience helps define everything about the business and the entire brand itself.

I encourage you to stop right now and make a list of questions about who your customers should be. For example:

1. What is my customer's average age?
2. Are they predominantly male or female?
3. What is their average income?
4. If the customer avatar has kids, are they into sports?
5. What kind of sports are their kids into?

Ask a lot of questions, and search for the answers to those questions. Then you can begin to build the perfect customer avatar. With a customer avatar, you will know how to get your target audience, how to talk to them, and how to create a relationship and connection with them.

HOW TO FIND YOUR AUDIENCE USING FACEBOOK AUDIENCE INSIGHTS

Facebook offers a tool called Audience Insights. It is at everyone's disposal, and it doesn't cost anything. This tool can help you research your customer.

Audience Insight allows you to learn a lot about people and their habits not just because of what they do on Facebook. Facebook has partnered with several third-party providers, and these third-party providers are the same people who would do telemarketing surveys back in the day. The information you gather will help you put together an idea of where your target audience is and who they associate with.

When you run Audience Insight studies, you can request to see, for example, women ages 25 to 54 in Nashville, Tennessee. It will show you their income levels, how many of them rent a home, the size of their household, the types of webpages that they like, etc. Those are great indicators of the things that they are interested in.

For instance, the online activity of your target customers may show you that there is a certain TV show many of them watch. If you have the right budget, you may determine that you want to get some airtime before and after that television show.

If you don't want to do that, then you do have to sit down with marketing professionals from these different industries. You would need to talk to a couple of different radio stations, TV stations, and outdoor companies. They would give you demographic information about their industry and the people who are watching, listening, or reading whatever those platforms offer.

I encourage you to do use Audience Insights because it allows you to put together an idea of your market in your area, your region, or maybe even nationally. You will start to see a lot about your demographic. That will help you build a plan and strategy to make sure that you know where your target market exists and even the correct channel to get started.

Advertising is, of course, important because advertise is the final design. It's the last layer that speaks to the customer, that tells them what you have.[26]

– TOM FORD

26 Tom Ford quote. (n.d.). Retrieved November 30, 2015, from
    http://www.brainyquote.com/quotes/quotes/t/tomford613735.html

Chapter 5

THE RIGHT MEDIA

The right media is just as important if not even more important than the actual message that you communicate through the different media channels.

The first thing you have to understand is who and where your customers are. What do they do? What do they read? What do they listen to while they drive?

Often when I coach people, I find that they have not processed these questions. They have not asked themselves whether or not they are using the correct channel to get their target market. Instead, they choose one channel or the other based on their personal interest. Or perhaps someone sold them some marketing on a specific one. But they haven't asked themselves the question: "Am I using the correct channel to get to my target market?"

Using the correct channel is one of the building blocks of spreading your message. You could have the greatest message in the world and a very well made campaign, but if you use the incorrect channel to spread it, it will still fail.

Approximately 20 years ago, I owned a party-supply business with a couple of locations in Birmingham, Alabama. One day, I woke up and felt like utilizing billboards to spread the message about my stores. I found the information for the outdoor companies that had most of the billboards in Birmingham, and I began talking to them. At that time, I didn't have the knowledge and understanding that I have today when it comes to marketing. I wasn't asking myself the question: "Are billboards the correct channel to get my target?"

I wanted to utilize billboards out of ego; I just wanted to see our name on those big boards because I thought it would look cool. I also thought it would make my friends, family, and those in the community who knew me think that we had arrived. Making sure that we were utilizing the correct source to talk to a potential audience so that we could grow our business was not my concern. I was simply looking at it as a means to have our name in the limelight because I knew a lot of people would see it – as if that mattered.

When I sat down with the sales professionals from those billboard companies, none of them asked me if it was the right avenue for getting our word out there. They had a job to do, and their job was to sell advertising for those billboard companies, so they simply showed me the rates and terms and how it worked. They weren't interested in what results the campaign would yield us.

Not every campaign needs to be connected to a direct return on investments. Larger companies and some other industries need market-share awareness. One of the ways to get that is to use some of the mass mediums, and outdoor and billboard advertising are such means.

However, for the majority of small and medium-sized companies, every single marketing dollar has to make a difference; every dollar has to grow the business from a monetary perspective. For that reason, it is critical to know where your target market is. Perhaps billboards are a perfect way to reach your target. Understanding which marketing channels suit your business and target audience is one of the biggest pieces of the puzzle of building your business.

The following is a list of several of the media channels or platforms available. Some of them are obvious while others may be less so. Maybe a couple of them would be right for you.

T V

Nearly every demographic watches TV at some level. Some of the questions you should ask are:

- What are they watching?
- Which channel are they watching?
- For how long are they watching?
- What are they doing when they are watching?

It doesn't matter what the demographic is. The question is: What demographic utilizes what channels, and what types of providers are they watching?

Say your target market is men at the ages 18 to 34. There is a good chance that you could sit down with your local cable or satellite provider, tell them what your demographic is, and look at some potential sports channels. To keep costs down and be cost-effective, you could look at some of the sports channels that don't reach the largest audience. To keep down your costs further, you could avoid channels such as ESPN and Fox Sports. You could even look at the times of the day that are non-prime times.

Let's take another example. Let's say your target audience is women between the ages 25 to 54. Perhaps your target audience is stay-at-home moms. Then you would make sure that you are on channels that have programs for kids. This way, TV might be a good place for you to spread your message.

NEWSPAPER

We all know that the newspaper is a dying breed because of computers, smartphones, tablets, and such. However, your target market may be using the paper more than you would think. For instance, if you are a higher-end jewelry store, there is a great chance that your target market is still reading the paper.

Depending on the size of the market you live in, the paper can be expensive. But if you live in a small town or community, the local community paper is a very affordable option that many read.

For instance, I live in the suburbs in Nashville, Tennessee. Where we live, there is a free community paper that comes to our mailbox every Wednesday. It's small, but we look through it every week, and it keeps us updated on the current events in our community. That is a great place for small businesses in and around that area to create consistent awareness. It's usually very affordable as well.

RADIO

I'm biased to the radio because I have sold radio airtime for several different media companies over the years. Radio allows you to broadcast your message in a frequent and consistent manner.

If you are not careful, radio, like TV, can be expensive. However, there are a lot of niche formats that can keep down your costs. These will have a lower amount of listeners, but they might reach those who you are looking for a lot better than the largest station in your market. Typically, there is always one that will fit your needs to connect with your target.

As a small business, you want to find the station where your target is, start small, and build your way into a long-term commitment to that station. If you do that, you will almost become a household name to that group of listeners.

If you advertise on radio, TV, or in the paper for just a few months, you are probably wasting your money. The exception is if you invest a significant amount of money for a dedicated, direct-return-on-investment campaign, which is hard to do without having a lot of experience.

Radio can be a great resource. If you own a small retail business, for instance, a flower shop or an automotive oil change store, radio could be a good marketing channel, provided that you use one that matches your demographic well. That is the secret ingredient.

If you have a larger budget, and you are, for example, an automotive dealer with several dealerships in your market, your situation is different. Then you can probably afford and need to be on large stations with large budgets and a very specific, dedicated campaign.

OUTDOOR

As I mentioned in my personal story earlier, I believe outdoor advertising can work. It's obvious that it works for a lot of people. However, it is a misused medium. For instance, many billboards are very cluttered. They have a lot of words, and half the time you can't even make them out because you only have a few seconds to catch the message. The best billboards have six or at most seven words (and that's a stretch).

An even better strategy is to use images that focus back to your target market. For instance, again, let's say you are a jewelry store. If it's close to Christmas or Valentine's Day, you could have an image of someone proposing on your billboard. That lets your target market think, "That looks like me." That is the subconscious thought that you want people to process from an image. You want them to connect with it. When they do, they will begin to connect with your brand in a deeper way. A lot of text, such as addresses and phone numbers, is hard to remember in such a short amount of time.

For a small business, I usually don't recommend outdoor advertising, unless there is a very specific fixed billboard close to a stop sign or red light where people stop for a much longer period. The reason I don't typically recommend billboards for small business is that it's harder to know whether or not their target demographic passes by every day. Just because 300,000 people pass by a billboard, that doesn't mean anything. If it's not the right 300,000 people, then you may waste your money.

I did not go through that thought process years ago when I wanted to do my billboards. I didn't ask: "Who are the 300,000 people passing by every day?" I was just mesmerized by the fact that a lot of people were going to see our name. I thought that in itself was going to help drive results, but that is simply not the case. If it's not the right people passing, the amount doesn't matter. You have to know for a fact that there are enough of your customers passing by the billboard for it to make sense.

UNIQUE OUTDOOR/TRANSIT

What I mean by unique is that you have other types of outdoor opportunities such as the sides of buses and the benches at the bus stops. Enclosed bus stops with roofs often have sides where there will be opportunities to put advertisements. There are also opportunities in parking garages and other buildings that use similar types of wrap that the automotive industry is using to wrap the vehicle.

In addition, there are places like the back of hotel room keys. The back of a hotel room key is very interesting. If you, for instance, have a pizza shop located within a couple of miles of several hotels, and especially if it is near an interstate, then that would be a no-brainer marketing strategy.

When people travel, especially when they get in late at night, they don't want to take the time to get in the car and go somewhere. If they see your advertisement on the back of their hotel room key as they check in, there is a great chance that you will get a return on that investment quite quickly.

If you own a pizza shop, sub shop, or any business in that type of food industry, and you are near express hotels where the nightly rates are around $100 per night, then that is a great place to be in front of. That target market is hungry and tired. They want to get fed, and they don't want to work a lot for it.

There are all kinds of unique outdoor type of marketing mediums to use. The question always remains: "Is this the right medium for me?" Maybe the outdoor and transit is for you, and maybe it isn't. You have to make the choice.

DIRECT MAIL/CATALOGS AND LEAFLETS

Direct mail advertising has been around for decades. At one point, it was one of the most popular ways to do specific, dedicated return-on-investment campaigns and direct-response campaigns. Due to the increased digital usage over the years, some would say that it's trailed off.

However, according to a study from 2012 from an online marketing institute, the average response rate for a direct mail campaign was around 4.4%.[27] That is significantly higher than email marketing. But you have to take into consideration the cost of the paper, printing, and postage. Direct mail can be extremely pricey in some cases. Because of the costs associated with this type of marketing, your cost per lead may be significantly higher than email marketing. However, that is not always the case. It depends on the campaign. You have to lay out the pros and cons and see what type of direct mail responses would be the right channel for you.

Some would say that the reason that direct mail is so much higher performing than email marketing is that there has been less competition over the years in the "snail mail" mailbox because of the rise of digital marketing

---

27 Beasley, L. (2013, June 13). Why Direct Mail Still Yields the Lowest Cost-Per-Lead and Highest Conversion Rate - Online Marketing Institute. Retrieved November 19, 2015, from http://www.onlinemarketinginstitute.org/blog/2013/06/why-direct-mail-still -yields-the-lowest-cost-per-lead-and-highest-conversion-rate/

and email campaigns. Since there is less competition in the mailbox, it's easier to be seen.

However, over the last year or so and certainly in the next 12 to 18 months, most predict that people will recognize that they can go back to the mailbox since there is less competition. I have seen an increase in the last 6 to 12 months. I have even seen that the way they do it is different. Lately, I have received some of the largest mailers I have ever seen in the mail because they are trying to get our attention.

Direct mail is a great tool, provided that it is the right place for you to be and that you do it correctly. Like billboards, one of the ways the medium is misused is by having too much text. When you look through your mail, and you see a lot of confusing and complicated text, you don't want to read it. Then what do you do with it? File 13, right in the trash can.

Unlike email marketing, you can't easily correct a direct mail campaign if it doesn't work. You could spend tens of thousands of dollars, and you may have missed a couple of pieces of it. Maybe you included too much text and not the right images, or you didn't time it right. But now you have spent the money, and it is what it is.

The advantage of email marketing is that you can see where a campaign went wrong before you launch it, and it doesn't cost very much to change it.

DIGITAL/ONLINE

More than ever before, you can get great results with different types of online advertising. One approach is to pay to be on specific niche sites. If we look at the target demographic of men at the ages 18 to 34 again, then some obviously niches would be sites that are related to cars or sports.

Or you can jump into what is called PPC, which is the pay-per-click game with Google, Yahoo, and others. PPC is extremely popular and highly effective if used properly. The problem is that there are a lot of people who don't know how to use this media channel correctly. They flirt with it a little bit, and when they don't achieve the success they were hoping for, they determine that it is not for them. It is partly because though it has been around for a while, it is still a relatively new channel for the small business community. It is still in a test phase, and many people have not seen the results that they look for. The reason for that is usually that their campaigns are not set up correctly.

If you are interested in this type of channel, and you believe that your target market is on the Internet (and there is a good chance that they are), then it might be a good channel for you. You have to make that decision. If this is the right type of channel for you, then I would highly recommend that you hire someone to help you. It could be someone from a marketing company, or it could even be a marketing individual who has good experience with the results that can help you.

You need to understand how and why PPC can work for you. It can be a great resource. It is proven to have excellent results for a lot of different industries. You can pinpoint geographies, industries, and keywords. That is one of the reasons why it has become such a successful platform.

SOCIAL MEDIA

There is a host of different platforms when it comes to social media: Twitter, LinkedIn, Facebook, and many others. For me, there is no question that Facebook is the darling of all social media platforms when it comes to advertising. You can use Facebook to gain fans and engage and interact, and that is something that you should do.

From an advertising perspective, you are shooting yourself in the foot by not utilizing Facebook as a daily marketing tool because the targeting ability is amazing. Not only can you target your specific audience by, for example, their interest, but you can also target people who visit your website. You can send a specific advertisement to people who visit your website. You can even decide to send an advertisement to people who have visited your website just today, just this week, or for the last 30 days. Or you can send a specific advertisement to people who are on your email list. If you have an email list, you can upload it to your Facebook account. Facebook will match up those emails with the emails of the account users on Facebook, and it will allow you to market to those people.

You can target people who look at your website and click on a specific page of your website. Maybe you have an event, and people are clicking on the event, but they don't sign up. You can send a separate advertisement to those who went to your webpage but did not sign up. That is how detailed this channel allows you to be.

You can even create a lookalike audience based on the people who like your Facebook page. Let's say you have 500 or 1,000 people who like your Facebook page. By running a lookalike audience, Facebook goes in and does a matchup in your area, the whole United States, or wherever you choose. They will find those who are similar to the people who like your page. Then you can run advertising just to them.

One of the biggest benefits of Facebook is the cost. You can start with as little as $5 a day. If you test a campaign, and it doesn't work, you can stop it. You can change it. You can edit it. You can increase it. Whatever you want to do, you can do it very easily with this medium. The cost to get in front of thousands on Facebook is minimal compared to almost every other medium, especially the mass approaches like TV, outdoor, radio, and the newspaper.

Compare it to resources like Pandora, for instance. Pandora offers a great opportunity to advertise, even as a local business, and it does very well. However, you have to start with a minimum budget of at least $5,000. You have to write a check to Pandora for that sum right off the bat, whether it goes well or poorly. With Facebook, you don't have to do that. You can start with $5 a day on Facebook, running the campaign for two or three days. If it is not working, you can change it or do whatever you have to do. It's one of the lowest cost investments around, and it can hit almost any target market.

We've looked at a lot of different opportunities in different media channels. Just like this chapter is titled, you have to use *the right media for your business.* You can't afford to use a medium just because you like it. You can't afford to advertise on radio stations just because it's your radio station that you listen to every single day. It may not be the radio station that your customers listen to. You can't put up your name on a billboard just because it's the billboard that you pass every day, and you happen to like it. That does not matter if your customers are not passing the same billboard. You can't send direct mail to a lot of people if they don't live in the ZIP Codes of where your customers are. You can't do pay-per-click advertising on the Internet if you don't use the keywords that your customers are interested in. You simply have to make sure that you are using the right media, and the right media is different for everybody.

Which media is right also depends on the size of your budget. You may be in an industry where you are a smaller business, and one of your competitors is 10 times your size. Guess what? They can do more than you. That is just the way it is. Just because you see that your competitor has 10 billboards, it doesn't mean that you should invest in that.

You can put yourself out of business if you don't properly set up your strategy to use the right media. Once you use a suitable media channel, you can get into the game of building your business on a consistent level. As your business grows, add another media channel and another media channel. Over time, you will build a successful business because you chose to ask the question: "Am I using the correct channel to get to my target market?"

Leadership is not about a title or a designation. It's about impact, influence and inspiration. Impact involves getting results, influence is about spreading the passion you have for your work, and you have to inspire team-mates and customers.[28]

– ROBIN S. SHARMA

---

28 Robin S. Sharma quote. (n.d.). Retrieved November 30, 2015, from http://www.brainyquote.com/quotes/quotes/r/robinssha628747.html

Chapter 6
THE RIGHT LEADERSHIP

As a kid, I always enjoyed being a part of the big picture, solving problems, and leading the way. Even then, it was not in my nature just to watch others make the decisions. I wanted to be a part of that process.

At that time, I didn't understand that those tendencies were a part of me wanting to be in leadership positions. It was a natural fit and feeling for me to adapt to those situations. I got deeply engaged in problem solving, even when there were many unknowns about what was going on.

As I got older, I recognized what leadership truly was. John Maxwell said, "Leadership is influence, nothing more nothing less."[29]

I'm very proud to be a founding member of The John Maxwell Team. John Maxwell is an expert author on the subject of leadership. He has written nearly 75 books over the last 20 to 25 years. His morals, values, and perspective on life line up closely to mine. I'm very fortunate and excited to be a part of his organization, and I continue to learn about leadership and how it applies to my world and my life.

The older that I have gotten, the more I have understood about what "influence" really means. People don't realize that we lack a significant amount of leadership in our culture today. Any given day, you can read about the lack of moral and values-based leaders in the news. It applies to our religious communities as well as political communities. We can see the results that come from people in powerful positions who have turned to greed and ego.

Just because someone has a title of CEO, Manager, or whatever it may be, it doesn't automatically make that person a leader. A leader is an influencer.

29 7 Factors that Influence Influence. (2013, July 8). [Web log post]. Retrieved November 18, 2015, from http://www.johnmaxwell.com/blog/7-factors-that-influence-influence

Someone in a non-managerial or non-decision-making role can have a lot of influence in an organization and be the actual person at the top of the chain. That is because influence ultimately is leadership, and the person with the influence ultimately can be the person who is leading.

There are a lot of business owners and entrepreneurs who don't see themselves as leaders and may never have realized their role as leaders. While some people are born with leadership talent, and some people want to take on that role in a natural setting, leadership can be taught. It is something that you can continue to refine and build upon.

It is important that we see leadership as something that we continue to develop. When we understand that we are influencing others in a way that can cause action, we want to continue to refine ourselves so that the action that we influence is positive.

CHARACTERISTICS OF A LEADER

To find out if you have a natural tendency as a leader, you can begin by looking at your personal experiences. What is happening in your personal life and your professional life? How are you responding to those experiences, whether they are good, bad or indifferent issues? If you look at them and examine them, you can tell pretty quickly where you stand in the role of a leader.

Leaders initiate while followers respond. Leaders are action-oriented. They notice when a problem is arising, and they make quick decisions to solve that problem. Followers, on the other hand, are not even aware that a problem is developing. Therefore, they are constantly in reaction mode.

If you look at whatever is going on in your personal life or professional life, where do you fit in those two equations? Do you tend to be action-oriented and results-oriented, or do you always tend to be in a reaction mode; always having to fix problems that happened because there wasn't enough planning involved ahead of time?

Maybe you are in an organization, and you are trying to figure out who is at the center of leadership. They are typically easy to find. Any time a situation arises, you can see the people who don't want to be a leader because they fall backward; they don't want to be involved in making a decision. On the other hand, there are those who step up to the plate and say: "I'll take on the task of problem-solver," or: "I want to be in charge of pushing this forward." Those are typically leaders.

You may be interested in leadership, but it may be difficult for you. Wherever you are right now, you can ask yourself: "Am I developing myself as a leader and stepping up to the plate? Am I solving problems and influencing others in a positive way that creates significance?"

Most leaders are willing to do the things that others are unwilling to do. A lot of people do not want to have any responsibility tied to issues. They don't want to be dragged through the mud. They don't want the extra work involved with the decisions or results that come through tough decisions or problem solving relational issues.

DEVELOPING YOUR LEADERSHIP SKILLS

If you want to develop yourself as a leader, you have to be willing to do things that most people are unwilling to do. That is usually how success is created. Successful people are willing to go far beyond what others are not willing to do.

If you don't feel like you can step up, or you just don't want to, then you probably need to have a paradigm shift in your thoughts. You need to begin thinking like a leader, buckle down, and start making some tough decisions that push you out of your comfort zone.

Recently, there was an article in *Forbes Magazine* that discussed 10 areas that point out why you may not be a leader. A couple of them rose to the top and made a lot of sense to me. One area was:

You care about process more than people: But for the people there is no platform. Without the people you have nothing to lead. When you place things above the people you lead you have failed as a leader.[30]

Both in organizations and people's personal life, many people stick to the processes regardless of how these processes affect others. If they do so, they do not show leadership qualities. If you are more committed to the processes of what goes on in your world than caring about the people involved, then

---

30 Myatt, M. (2013, January 23). Why You're Not A Leader. Retrieved November 17, 2015, from http://www.forbes.com/sites/mikemyatt/2013/01/23/why-youre-not-a-leader/

I challenge you to shift your thinking and care more about the people. The processes can change depending on the people you have on the bus.

The other thing that resonated with me in the article in *Forbes* was where it said:

> **You follow the rules instead of breaking them:** Status quo is the great enemy of leadership. Leadership is nothing if not understanding the need for change, and then possessing the ability to deliver it.[31]

I'm not suggesting that we should just be rule-breakers and go against the natural flow. What I mean is that if you are going to maintain status quo, then you are not willing to do what good quality leaders will do. Good quality leaders will always ask the question: Just because we have always done this, does that means that we have to do it? There are many different examples.

For instance, years ago when Apple created the first smartphone, we were all amazed at this device and what it could do. It introduced us to the app world. It excited us. We were as curious about what would come next. Now, there is competition from other developers. It shows us that technology moves our culture at a very fast speed. What is interesting is that users like myself hold these devices and say: "Man, I wish this device could do this or do that." We are moving at such a fast pace that good leaders have to stay in front and be willing to adapt and change to prevent them from just being status quo.

If you look at a giant Fortune 500 Company like McDonald's, you can't help but see that their leadership has made some tough and aggressive decisions to stay relevant. McDonald's is no longer only a burger-and-fries type of restaurant. They have added the McCafé to stay relevant and competitive to new chains like Panera Bread and Starbucks. They no longer just want to sell you hamburgers and French fries. They want to be a part of your life and your community. They have been willing to do what their competitors, such as Burger King and Wendy's, have not yet done (for the most part). The latter companies are far behind. The flow has changed, and McDonald's has adapted.

---

31   Myatt, M. (2013, January 23). Why You're Not A Leader. Retrieved November 17, 2015, from http://www.forbes.com/sites/mikemyatt/2013/01/23/why-youre-not-a-leader/

You have to ask yourself: Am I willing to break the rules, go out of my comfort zone, and begin to make decisions to continue to move forwarded to be competitive?

While there are many different ways to continue developing yourself as a leader, three keys stand out to me.

Key 1: Read and then read some more. Reading is the backbone of continuing to build your education regardless of what topic you try to develop yourself in, especially leadership. There are more books and publications available on the topic of leadership than ever. They will expand your thought and horizon on leadership.

A study in 2009 found that reading actually helps us to create new neural pathways, as our brains process the experiences that we read about. This does not occur from watching television, playing computer games or engaging in other passive activities.

Another fascinating study from the University of Sussex in 2009 found that a mere six minutes of reading can reduce stress levels by more than two-thirds. They found that this amount of reading was even more beneficial than listening to music or going for a walk.[32]

Let's think about that for a moment. Say you invest even as little as six minutes of reading a day on the subject of leadership from proven leaders. They have gone before, paved the way, and are now well ahead, and they are bringing new thought to the subject. If you spend just six minutes a day expanding your thoughts, that is an obtainable and very easy way to continue developing yourself as a leader.

Key 2: Take bold risks. I'm not suggesting that you put yourself in financial loss for the sake of risk. I simply recommend that you take risks and push yourself out of your comfort zone. Once you do, you begin to learn a lot about yourself and what your weaknesses and your strengths are, especially when you do it with others around you.

Remember, influence is true leadership. We take risks. We make decisions that affect other people. It pushes us to communicate with others around us, whether they are family, coworkers, employees, vendors or customers.

---

32 http://goodworldnews.org/index.php/health/item/277-studies-show-reading-is
-good-for-your-health

It pushes us into a new area of communication that can be challenging. But without that risk, we won't be able to work on the areas that we have not pushed to the limits yet.

A lot of people want to make everything perfect before they launch a new product or send out an email campaign. Or they want to have everything perfect before they start offering a new line of products to their customers. The reality is that sometimes you have to take a risk and start selling yourself despite the possibility of embarrassment and mistakes. We certainly want to do excellent work and plan as best we can, but sometimes we have to take some risks to push ourselves out of the comfort zone.

Key 3: Learn to prioritize. Great leaders understand where their time should be spent. We live in a world where we are flooded with email, text messages, and notifications from LinkedIn, Facebook, Instagram, Twitter, whatever it maybe. We spend our time just bouncing between all these different places. Great leaders understand how to prioritize their time.

Richard Koch has written a book called *The 80/20 Principle*. In this book, he goes deep into the discussion of how to achieve more with less. The book is based on the Pareto's principle, which is that 20% of your priorities will give you 80% of your production if you spend your time, energy, and money on the top 20% of your priorities. Great leaders dig deep into knowing where their time is best spent to give them the best results possible.

While there are many different ways, the three keys that we just discussed can significantly help you. They don't cost you any money to do, and they can help you continue to evolve yourself and develop yourself as a leader.

Most people want to wave the magic wand and snap their fingers to become a leader. It's just not that simple. Leadership is a journey; it's not a destination. Leadership is something that continues to form around you the older you get, with the different experiences you have, and with the people who are around you.

One thing is for sure: You have to continue to develop yourself on a daily basis, continue to invest in yourself, and continue to surround yourself with people who you can trust. The more you do it, the better you get at it, and the more impact you will make on your community and the world.

Based on my pool of coached clients, 90% of the challenges for business owners exist in a lack of personal development.[33]

– DARREN L JOHNSON

---

33   Darren L Johnson quote. (n.d.). Retrieved November 30, 2015, from http://www.brainyquote.com/quotes/quotes/d/darrenljoh601629.html

Chapter 7

THE RIGHT MENTOR

Many people ask: "Why do I need to have a mentor or a business coach?" There are plenty of business owners, business professionals, and entrepreneurs who believe that they have everything figured out and that their decisions are the best decisions. They don't often consider the need to have outside input on what they do.

However, a business coach or mentor is an excellent resource for anyone who values growth in any industry. If you dig a little, you learn that those who experience rapid growth typically have a mentor, a business coach, or some type of adviser. That is why it's important.

Believe it or not, we don't know everything. It is very difficult to make all the decisions necessary for strategic and productive growth. It is especially challenging to do that without having outside input from someone who either has been there before or is connected to a lot of people who are seeing results. In a mentoring relationship, you can draw off the other person's experiences.

I would have given anything to know this key a little over 20 years ago. A few years after I had started my party-supply business back in the mid-90s, I purchased a brand new vehicle, a truck, and I loved it. While I was in the parking lot picking up the car, I ran into somebody I knew. This person called my name and came over. We began talking, and he looked at my car and said: "Man, this truck is beautiful. Your business must be doing well." I'll never forget that because, at that moment, my business was not doing well. From the outside, I gave off the impression that we were quite successful, but that was not the case in reality. We were struggling, and many of the decisions that I had been making were not working.

At the time, I was unable and unwilling to be open and vulnerable to anyone. I told myself that I knew what I was doing. I was very young – in my early 20s – and I had not been down the road of experience at that time. I believed that it would turn around and that I knew what I was doing.

I wish I would have known about the importance and the value of having a business coach and a mentor who could have walked through those things with me. Then I could have received help to see things I could not, which would have helped me in my decision-making and probably saved my business at that time.

I would also have saved a lot of money and countless hours of indecisiveness trying to figure out what I should do in my specific circumstances. I even spent a lot of money on advertising that I should have never spent simply because I thought it was the right thing to do. Had I had someone speak into my life and business, they would have stopped me and told me that I should not spend that kind of money. They would have let me know that my business was not big enough yet, or that it was not my industry, or that my types of products and services did not serve well for that platform or media.

Do you feel like that in your business? Do you feel like that in the role that you play in what you do? Do you feel like you constantly second guess yourself or have a lot of uncertainties that prevent you from either making swift decisions or even making the right decision? Maybe you are even making decent decisions, but things have plateaued.

If you feel that way, and you just cross your fingers and hope for the best when you make decisions, then you are a perfect candidate to seek input or advice from a mentor or a coach.

Maybe your business is growing and doing very well at the moment. I remember working with a great medium-sized business in Florida, and they told me their situation. They had grown quickly and were doing all the right things. But when the economy collapsed, they, like most business, were not set up to handle the consequences, so they nearly lost their business. Thankfully, they managed to save it, but they had to make a lot of changes. They had to let go of many employees and rearrange their structure, and they lost a lot of money. They realized that they had been spending money frivolously and that they had a lot of wasted space in the facilities they rented. They believed that they could have seen some of these issues and prevented some of the fallout that they went through if they had had someone to speak into their business.

Business owners and entrepreneurs work inside the business. Since a business coach, mentor, or adviser doesn't spend a lot of energy inside the business, they will have a different perspective because they can offer advice from outside the business.

By adviser, coach, or mentor, I don't mean a family member or neighbor. It's fine to have those as a sounding board. However, an adviser, coach, or mentor should fully understand business and marketing. They need to have experienced it before at some level. Then they can help you navigate the decisions that you have to make for your particular purpose. You need people who have been down that road to some degree so that you can learn from the mistakes that they have made. It's important to have people who have gone through challenging periods that you can draw from. They can encourage you because they have been there and are now on the other side.

Those people don't have to be in your specific industry. Many different business models and experiences can transfer from one business model to another or one industry to another.

Any business, large or small, can hire a business coach or a mentor. Realtors, dentists, and sales managers can all have a mentor or business coach who speaks into the daily process and the overall scope and goals of their particular business.

The reason that someone turns to a coach or a mentor is to get fresh perspectives on ways to accomplish their goals. Business coaches can often be the voice of reason, someone who can pull you through situations that are extremely challenging. Or they can talk you off the ledge of rather stupid ideas or decisions such as the ones I made back in the day. Anyone who has an open mind can benefit from the assistance of a mentor or coach. Small business, big business, and succeeding or failing businesses can all benefit, as long as they are open-minded.

Think about world athletes today. For instance, Tiger Woods has multiple swing coaches. You could argue: "Sure, he has coaches. He has the money to provide that," but I'm not suggesting that you spend six figures on a coach. Tiger Woods should and needs to do so because he has products and services that he endorses, and he make millions in an industry where that is the way it works.

The point is that even though he has been viewed as one of the best golfers in the world, he still has coaches. Those around him speak into what he does, and that is why it is incredibly important. The game of golf is getting highly competitive, and to stay competitive and relevant, you must have people around you who understand what is going on.

My son, who is 15 years old, is on his high school's golf team. We have gone through coaching programs, camps, and individual coaches with him. I will never forget when he had the individual coach. What he learned and what I watched him learn through just those first few 60-minute lessons was incredible. Most people think that you just get out and hit a golf ball with a stick. However, unless someone who understands the techniques and has the experience teaches you, you will never reach the top. There are different strategies for how to play in certain kind of conditions: when the grass is wet, when the grass is extremely dry, when there are clouds overhead, and when there are heavy downpours. You have to seek the help of somebody who knows what to do. Their experience can help you improve and make better decisions.

Another example is Celine Dion. Celine Dion has a vocal coach. Elite performers get to where they are and stay there because they have coaches or mentors who help them continue to be the best at what they do.

Presidents have advisers. They have whole cabinets. They should have that because they are making world-changing decisions. And they know that whatever decision they make, someone is going to love it, someone is going to hate it, and someone is going to detest it. For that reason, they always bounce their thoughts and decisions off of experienced people who have been in different roles in the political environment.

While you may not be a president, a world performer, or a top athlete, you still need to invest in someone who can help you in the trenches of the daily decisions to grow your business. Without that, it's going to be a challenge.

BENEFITS OF HAVING A MENTOR OR COACH

Increased productivity and income. Now, you may wonder how just having a coach or a mentor is going to increase your productivity and income. A coach or mentor will help you look at your day – what you do and how you do it. They can show you areas where you can maximize and get back some of your time. You can sit down and evaluate how are you accomplishing the tasks throughout your day. The coach or mentor will then begin to highlight areas where you can sometimes gain one, two, or three hours per day, and accomplish more with less time. That production should point to ways that you can increase the areas that are actionable items that product greater income potential. In one area alone, you could maximize your productivity. So stop wasting valuable time, and increase your effectiveness and influence in areas that are income-producing.

Many people, especially those of us who are entrepreneurs, spend our days doing many different tasks. But just because you are active and get a lot done, that doesn't mean that you do the right things or do it in the correct order. It doesn't mean that you are focused and pay attention to the specific areas that you know has greater income potential.

Accountability. There were some very specific decisions that I made in my past businesses that I did not succeed in. I wish I had someone there to say: "If you do that, you will lose a lot of money," but that person wasn't there.

Accountability will help you avoid those situations. You need someone who you can trust and be vulnerable with and open-minded toward. That way, when that person warns you that you are about to make a mistake or presents you with some possible positive and negative outcomes of your decision, you can evaluate those decisions. Maybe you are trying to hire a new employee for a particular part of your business or company. A mentor or a coach can help you evaluate whether or not that is the right person for the role.

People often hire people who are completely mismatched. They may have excellent skill sets, but because they try to get the job done quickly, they do not stop to ask if it's a right fit when it comes to personality. A coach or a mentor will ask you those type of questions. They help you dodge some monumental mistakes, which in turn will provide income generation for you.

Increased learning. You will be able to learn a lot because of the different perspectives that a coach can bring. The coach or mentor works with a lot of different people, industries of various sizes, and a variety of industries. Because of that, he or she is experienced and has knowledge in many different areas.

You can draw off of those perspectives because they are inside businesses of all kinds and sizes and meet with people who are new in business and people who have been in business for 20 years or more. They see good and bad ideas and profitable and unprofitable decisions. You can draw and learn from those perspectives and use them in your business.

Clarity on goal setting. If you have a certain goal structure that won't work, a coach can let you know that, and they can show you why. They can point out if it will be difficult to get there. They will help you structure your goals in a better way and create action steps associated with the goals that come to the overall desired result that you are after.

When you have a coach or mentor, and you begin to march through those goals, they are easier to get through, they have a better outcome, and you will see quicker and bigger results. That is because you have somebody on the outside who works with both you and many other people. They have been there. They have done it. For those reasons, they can help you find a less resistant way to get you where you want to be than you do if you sit down alone with little or no experience and with no influence or input from someone else.

Increased leadership skills. People often misunderstand their role as an entrepreneur, business owner, or business manager. You are working with people or for people, or people are working for you. Every single day, you have influence in people's lives.

Earlier, I quoted John Maxwell who said, "Leadership is influence, nothing more nothing less."[34] How are you influencing others? When you influence others, work with them and invest in their lives in the right way because that investment will come back to you. Then people will not view you as a positional leader – according to your title. Instead, they will begin to see that you utilize your position from an influence perspective to invest in people's lives.

Having a coach or a mentor will help you walk down that path. When you invest in influencing others, that growth will come back in ways that you can't anticipate. You will feel like that the sky is falling, and it is raining opportunities. That will happen as a result of the investment that you make in other people's lives.

Reassurance. Reassurance is different than accountability. We constantly come up with ideas and want to see if these ideas are going to work. Often, we are unsure if they will work. Think about how many times you have made a decision based on an idea, and you thought: "Well, we'll find out if this is going to work or not."

---

34   7 Factors that Influence Influence. (2013, July 8). [Web log post]. Retrieved November 18, 2015, from http://www.johnmaxwell.com/blog/7-factors-that-influence-influence

A coach or a mentor will provide you with perspective. They may say that it is a fantastic idea and may even make some suggestions on how you could improve it. Or they may point out some significant obstacles that you might encounter with the idea. Perhaps they will make you aware of something you didn't know, and you will avert a crisis and a waste of time, effort, and energy. That is why having a business coach or a mentor in your life will often help you identify whether or not an idea is a good one. It is an invaluable investment because, as entrepreneurs, the ideas are what make our business move forward. We will always make some mistakes, and that is fine. Even with a mentor or a coach, that is going to happen. But you can eliminate many of them by following the advice of somebody who is involved on a consistent basis.

The benefit of additional input in your life is tremendous. If you have never thought about seeking help from a mentor or a business coach, there is no better time than right now. There are people who are ready and willing to help. You don't have to spend thousands of dollars. Although, if the annual income of your business is $10 million, you should be investing significantly in advisers, mentors, or coaches. Or perhaps your annual income is less than $250,000. Then you have no business investing in a six-figure business coach. You can still consult with or get coaching with someone on a consistent basis.

Applying these strategies and getting invested with someone can be the difference in making your business succeed or getting it out of a rut, and taking it to a new level. It can help you go from mediocre to good, from good to great, and from great to amazing. That is all the difference that a business coach or a mentor can make in your business life.

We are all in the business of sales. Teachers sell students on learning, parents sell their children on making good grades and behaving, and traditional salesmen sell their products.[35]

– DAVE RAMSEY

35   Dave Ramsey quote. (n.d.). Retrieved November 30, 2015, from http://www.brainyquote.com/quotes/quotes/d/daveramsey520310.html

Bonus Chapter

THE RIGHT USP

We have now gone through seven key strategies, which I believe will create extraordinary growth if you spend time developing them.

Before we wrap things up, I wanted to give you a bonus chapter dedicated to creating a unique selling proposition. Earlier in the book, we discussed having *the right message*. Part of that message is a specific selling proposition that is unique to you. Once you have your message, you should incorporate your USP.

Having a unique selling proposition, or USP for short, is vital to any business whether it is a sole proprietor or a large company. Knowing the position that you have against your competitor is essential. It should be the foundation of any business, especially if you are in a competitive market, and most businesses have competitive flare somewhere along the way.

In coaching both small and medium-sized businesses, I often find that entrepreneurs are so eager to create their business and be the boss, if you will, that they fail to realize exactly where they should be and how they should be viewed by their customer-base.

A mistake that is often made in the process is that the business is created based on the personal preferences of a business owner, or perhaps the marketing director if there are partners in the business. They begin to make decisions about products and services for the business based on their personal needs, wants, or desires.

When I owned the party-supply business 20 years ago, my partner and I based the decisions of what types of products we should carry in our store on what we liked. We did not step back and ask: "Would our customers like this?" "Will the demographic that we're trying to attract like this?"

Not having a clear understanding of what our customers want can put us in a bad position. Then, if something in our business isn't selling well, we can't step back and make the excuse that our customers didn't like it. It can often leave us perplexed. We don't understand why the products aren't selling better than they are since we have great customer service and a great product. Without a unique selling proposition, you won't stand out next to the competition. Your USP makes your business valuable and special to your target audience. It is fundamental to describing who you are and what you do.

WHAT A USP IS NOT

Businesses often confuse a USP with a slogan. Slogans are important, but they are typically attached to an advertising campaign. A slogan is not designed specifically to separate yourself from your competition.

A USP is not your mission statement either. Mission statements are incredibly valuable, and you need them. Your USP can come from your mission statement as to who you are as an overall business, but it is not your mission statement.

It's certainly not your vision statement. Many businesses try to base their business on their visions and their core values, and you should. But that is not what will set you apart from your competitors when it comes to who you are and why you do what you do. A USP answers the question why someone should do business with you or why they should value your service over somebody else's. It allows the consumers to identify themselves with your business. The USP is usually attached to why and where someone is when it comes to identifying with the products.

Far too many businesses say that their USP is that they have great customer service or unbeatable prices. While those things may be true, those reasons can often be shallow. It doesn't ultimately, quickly, easily, and uniquely describe who you are as a business.

WHAT A USP CAN DO

In 1960, the car rental company Avis had been Number 2 in the market for many years, whereas Hertz had been Number 1. That year, Avis decided that they had to make some changes in their business. They turned to a high-end marketing agency for help to solve their problem of being Number 2 and having nowhere close to the volume that Hertz had.

A copywriter at the marketing firm that they hired created what is probably one of the most unique selling propositions around. The USP for Avis became: "We're number two; we try harder." What they were saying was: "We know that we're not number one. We know that Hertz is better than we are. Because of that, we are now going to do it better than they do."

Before the campaign launched in 1962, one of the co-founders of the firm said that if they were going to adopt this as their unique selling proposition, then they would have to stand behind what it said and meant. They couldn't use it if they had poor customer service, poor pricing, and a poor business structure. If they were going to say that they would try harder, then they would have to back up that claim.

Avis not only adopted it as a unique selling proposition for their business, but they became it. Their company, as well as their employees, rallied around the USP. Everyone in the organization joined in on the effort of doing what they did better than anybody else in their industry.

The results were staggering. Previously, Avis had been around $3 million or $4 million in the red. The very first year after creating that USP in 1962, they gained 11% of the market share and turned a profit of $1.2 million. It was the first time they had seen any profit in 13 years. By 1966, they ended up with 35% of the market share, and it all started with creating a unique selling proposition.

A USP can do a lot for businesses. While Avis had the luxury of hiring a high-end marketing firm, the principles apply to smaller businesses as well. When you set yourself apart from those who are in the same industry as you, you can target and hone in on people who are looking for your products or services. The USP will make you easier to find than if you are bland and don't have anything special about you.

The questions that businesses and entrepreneurs need to ask are:

- If you had a USP, how would it make you better?
- How would it position you differently than the next guy?
- What can you do to be different?
- If the USP made you different, are you going to live up the claims that it would make?

Businesses often use slogans saying something along the lines of: "We are the best in the county, and we have unbeatable prices." They are designed to make people believe it. However, most businesses can't fulfill such claims.

If you have a USP, you must be willing to do what Avis did; you have to stand behind it. Doing it correctly helps squelch unsubstantiated claims. Avis said that they would do it better, and we can see that people believed it and bought into it because of the increase in sales that followed.

A USP helps you define who your target customer is. Defining your target customer is crucial. For instance, it's easy for someone in the dental industry to say that their target customer is anybody who has teeth. Everyone may need dental work, and it's fair to make that statement. But it doesn't set you apart when you are not more specific about who you are and what you offer.

Say there are two buildings set side-by-side. On the front of one of the buildings, it says "Dentist" at the top. On the building right next to it, it also says "Dentist." If a consumer stands on the sidewalk and looks at both of those buildings, how is he or she supposed to tell one from the other? If one of them has a more distinct character than the other, then that is the one that will attract the consumer.

As a dentist, you can, for example, define yourself by choosing to be in pediatrics. You can even drill (no pun intended) down further by offering specialties within your field. You can do things that make you unique. Say your dental practice is located in an affluent area where the average household income is anywhere between $120,000 to $150,000. Then you could create your dental practice to be a spa-like treatment. The lobby could have a waterfall and a grand piano. While these features have nothing to do with dental work, they do speak to an affluent individual who will pay for that type of service and treatment. Doing such things sets you apart even as a dentist in the dental world.

Most people don't think that way, though. They just try to find the next customer, and they don't have a true clarity and identity. It's crucial that we define who our target audience is, and having a USP helps us do that. We have to take the time to think about who our target is and how we can position ourselves and our business to suit that target.

We have to understand that we must be defined for a specific customer regardless of our personal interest, whether we like it or not. Our preferences are not nearly as relevant as our customers'. Not only can your USP give you definition, but it also allows you to make an implied promise to your market.

A great USP becomes who you are. Avis' USP became who they are. They became the fact that they were going to try harder. They embraced that as an entire company. That is the difference between slogans and USPs. Slogans are attached to a marketing campaign that may have some value, but they are limited. A USP becomes who they are. It's the product of the overall mission and vision of the company.

If you don't have a unique selling proposition, and you want to have one, you may take out a pen and paper and start to write down some things. You have to take the time to make sure that the proposition you create is what is best for your company today.

Your proposition can change, and it needs to change from time to time. Avis held onto theirs for 50 years, but eventually they had to adopt a different direction because they found themselves in the same hole that they had been in 50 years prior. Don't rush trying to figure it out. Don't just try to be clever, fun, or catchy either. Catchy is irrelevant if it's not going to produce any results. A unique selling proposition is all about setting yourself apart from your competitors to create results.

You have to take some time to identify those things that will make you different and more attractive than the next guy next door. That is why creating a USP and living by it is a foundational step in creating a strong business.

The USP should be everywhere so that your customers can see it, begin to know and understand it, and, most importantly, begin to believe it. That alone is something that will help you gain results in your business.

CONCLUSION

In this book, I have shared many different strategies and ways to help you grow your business. Your needs will depend on your business. Maybe you don't have a business yet, or maybe you have been in business for 20 years.

Some of the strategies that I have presented in this book, you can implement today. Other strategies, you may need to take some time and evaluate how they will work in your business environment.

However, if you do nothing, you will get exactly where you are right now. Taking action is by far one of the biggest obstacles every business owner and entrepreneur face.

We all say that we are going to do something. But those who have the discipline and dedication to take action are the ones who will be among the top 3% of entrepreneurs who earn the living that they want to earn.

Everyone wants to be successful. There is not a business owner, marketing director, entrepreneur, or sales professional in the world who will start out by saying: "I don't want to be successful. I want to be mediocre."

Everyone I know wants to make a good living. And there is nothing wrong with that. But few people who say that take the required steps to get there and have the discipline necessary to make it work.

It is not easy. It is not for the fainthearted. Most people go into business ownership and learn very quickly that is one of the hardest things to do. That is why, according to the Small Business Administration, 80% of businesses fail in their first year.[36] I understand that. I have been there. The failure is typically due to lack of knowledge and drive to take the correct action necessary.

You may only be able to apply one of these strategies that we have discussed. But if you do that, you are taking your next step towards getting to

36   Wagner, E. (2013, September 12). Five Reasons 8 Out Of 10 Businesses Fail. Retrieved November 19, 2015, from http://www.forbes.com/sites/ericwagner/2013/09/12/five-reasons-8-out-of-10-businesses-fail/

where you want to go. Maybe you can apply two, three, four, or five strategies. Maybe there are 20 things in this book that you can do.

Whatever it may be, don't wait until it's too late. Start taking small measurable steps. Do the things required. You know where you are and all you do in your business. Start investing in yourself today by following these strategies.

I vividly remember a conversation I had many years ago in 1974, which marked a turning point in my leadership journey. I was sitting at a Holiday Inn with my friend, Kurt Campmeyer, when he asked me if I had a personal growth plan. I didn't. In fact, I didn't even know you were supposed to have one.[37]

– JOHN C. MAXWELL

37   John C. Maxwell quote. (n.d.). Retrieved November 30, 2015, from
http://www.brainyquote.com/quotes/quotes/j/johncmaxw600887.html

ABOUT THE AUTHOR

BJ O'Neal is a successful entrepreneur with more than 20 years experience in the world of traditional and digital media, business ownership, coaching, and more. As a founding partner and certified coach, teacher, and speaker with the John Maxwell Team, he helps businesses achieve success through strategic marketing, branding, and sales funnel techniques.

In addition, BJ has spent years working with radio stations across the country to expand their revue streams through integrative partnerships.

BJ lives just outside Franklin, TN, with his wife, DeAundra, and three kids. For coaching and speaking information, visit **www.bjoneal.com** or email to **bj@bjoneal.com**.

Made in the USA
Coppell, TX
03 February 2023

12071999R00049